"When you do things from your soul, you feel a river moving in you, a joy."

RUMI

The life of a man is a circle from childhood to childhood, and so it is in everything where power moves. Even the seasons form a great circle in their changing, and always come back again to where they were. The sun comes forth and goes down again in a circle. The moon does the same, and both are round. The wind, in its greatest power, whirls. Birds make their nests in circles, for theirs is the same religion as ours. The sky is round, and I have heard that the earth is round like a ball, and so are all the stars. Everything the Power of the World does is done in a circle.

"

BLACK ELK

happiness

COLOR *yourself* CALM

Mandalas by
Paul Heussenstamm

BARRON'S

Introduction

Happiness

Butterflies

Salmon

Dance of Abundance

Horseplay

Cat Lovers

Paradise

Deep Divers

Flight of the Ibis

Indian Turquoise

Jaded Tiger

Kavai

Magic Dancer

Spirit Dancing

Moon Over Georgia

Flower Power

Butterflies and Green Clouds

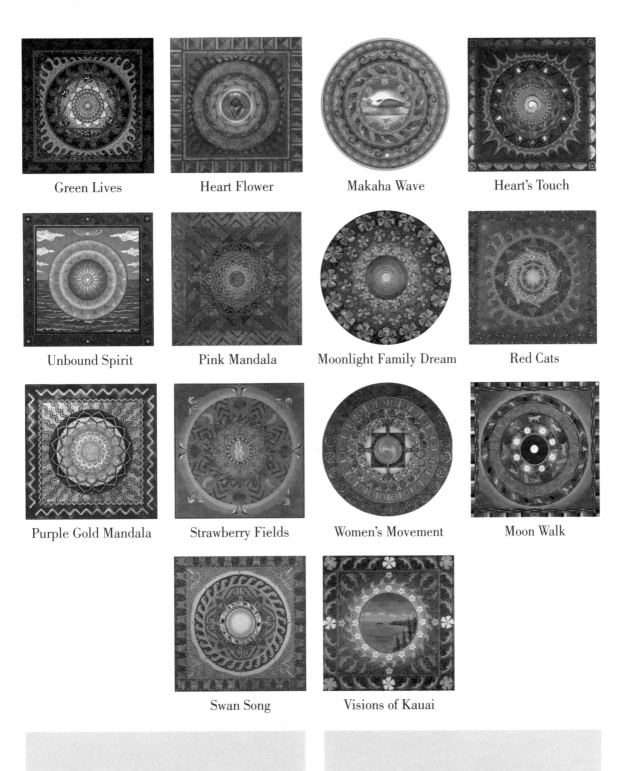

Green Lives

Heart Flower

Makaha Wave

Heart's Touch

Unbound Spirit

Pink Mandala

Moonlight Family Dream

Red Cats

Purple Gold Mandala

Strawberry Fields

Women's Movement

Moon Walk

Swan Song

Visions of Kauai

About the
quotes

About the
illustrator

INTRODUCTION

Welcome to the world of mandalas and the beginning of your journey to becoming more focused and centered by coloring your mind calm. This mindfulness-inspired coloring book includes 30 original color mandalas with their accompanying black-and-white templates to color in, which will expand your self-awareness and open the door into your own creativity.

Mandalas are an ancient form of meditative art. Simply put, the mandala is a design that draws your eye toward its center, which focuses your mind on the present moment and opens up your heart.

Within our fast-paced society, we are often in our minds rather than in our hearts—our minds then become closed to creativity, relaxation, or happiness. Once you begin to color in the mandalas, your center will begin to shift from your mind and into your heart. The core of the mandala then becomes the center of your heart. Importantly, once your heart is open your creativity naturally pours forth.

Coloring in mandalas relaxes the mind, body, and spirit; relieves stress; and is a chance to explore your own inner creativity. For the past 25 years, I have been exploring, painting, practicing, and teaching the art of mandala painting. The first thing you should know is that coloring mandalas requires no previous experience or innate artistic talent. As a teacher, the hardest task is to dispel the worries of students and banish any thoughts that they are not creative and are not naturally artistic.

The key to mandala coloring is to simply take the time to sit quietly, to focus your mind, and to begin coloring. This is precisely how I started my journey of coloring and painting mandalas way back in the late 1980s. At first, I did it for fun, but it then led to a profound change in my lifestyle. It makes no difference if you color in a single mandala or one thousand mandalas, it is merely the practice of centering yourself through creativity and relaxation, which ultimately leads to increased happiness.

Art is transformative. Mandala coloring transforms your attitude toward life and develops your consciousness. When you reach this meditative state through coloring, your body becomes more sensitive, your eyes see more deeply, and you will feel more intensely.

Congratulations on arriving at this point. You will now discover that as you begin to color in these mandalas your awareness will expand. As your awareness expands, and the more you color, you will begin to look and feel more deeply into the mandalas. Essentially, as you open up to see inside the mandala you are simultaneously opening up yourself.

A mandala is a very ancient guide that symbolically allows you to look into yourself. The process of coloring in a mandala can give you profound insights into your psyche and your mind. It appears simple, yet there are layers of growth, understanding, and even a transforming of consciousness that are revealed in a mandala painting, whether coloring one in or simply looking at one. The key to mandala meditation is to sit still and gaze at one. Once you have colored in several mandalas—or even several parts of one mandala—you will begin to feel and see patterns within yourself. This is deeply valuable because it allows you to recognize your own inner patterns and it helps you to communicate with your conscious self through the core patterns.

HAPPINESS

ACCEPTANCE

Participation in creative pursuits shifts your center from your mind to your heart, which increases your happiness. I have been teaching creative courses for the past 25 years and I always tell my students that when you take one of my workshops you must step outside of your conscious mind and open up your channels of creativity.

EXISTENCE

When you engage with this inner creativity, your otherwise narrow world is transformed into an infinite universe. When I am immersed in any creative process, I exist outside of time and space, but I equally feel incredibly connected to the universe as a whole.

CONNECTIVITY

On the deepest level, the artist is a conduit—the mandalas are paintings that are simply a passage for their creator. The beauty of creative pursuits is that once your heart is open and you are fully connected to the infinite universe, creativity naturally spills forth. Someone who has never considered himself/herself a creative can, in an instant, experience a shift in his/her existence.

TRANSFORMATION

Creativity can radically alter your perspective. The wonderful thing about coloring mandalas is that once you learn the practice, coloring is easily shareable with friends, with loved ones, and with children.

STILLNESS

When coloring mandalas, you can no longer think about blues, purples, or greens in the same way. Thoughts become colors. Colors become patterns. Patterns awaken the soul. Coloring becomes magic. From deep within, you will feel stillness and relaxation, because the colors shine through you. Your mind shifts from the logical and reasoning left brain to the intuitive and emotional right brain.

ATTAINMENT

As you begin to access your inner creativity, while also allowing yourself the time, patience, and focus to color yourself calm, your perspectives and outlook on life will change. Transformation is a form of happiness that wells up from your core being. This attainment of joy will most likely be beyond anything you have ever felt before.

TRANSMITTANCE

In becoming an artist, you are making something that you love, while also touching others on a very deep level. After you have colored in each of your chosen mandalas, take a photograph or scan your creation and share it on social media with the hashtag #coloryourselfcalm so that people all over the world can enjoy your creativity. This creates a form of shared happiness that no words can do justice.

Butterflies

Art is ecstasy to the soul.

Salmon

Dance of Abundance

"It is so simple after all, why should I hesitate to make all this gold and all this joy of the sun flow onto my canvas."
PAUL GAUGUIN

Horseplay

Cat Lovers

The universe sends paintings directly to my heart, and
then from my heart they dance onto my canvas.

Paradise

Deep Divers

There are no words for the true value of painting.
I feel it in my heart, my body, and my soul.

Flight of the Ibis

Indian Turquoise

When you start to paint a mandala, the magic and the ecstasy
of creating will soon become apparent.

Jaded Tiger

Kavai

A great painting achieves an emotion beyond bliss.

Magic Dancer

Spirit Dancing

"There is no way to happiness—happiness is the way."
THICH NHAT HANH

Moon Over Georgia

Flower Power

The artist creates his or her own universe. Mandala painting is a journey toward enlightenment beyond consciousness.

Butterflies and Green Clouds

Green Lives

"A work of art must also possess a soul and the power to shine forth."
MOTHER MEERA

Heart Flower

Makaha Wave

*"The mandala is an archetypal image whose occurrence is attested throughout
the ages. It signifies the wholeness of the Self. This circular image represents the
wholeness of the psychic ground, or to put it in mythic terms, the divinity of man."*
CARL JUNG

Heart's Touch

Unbound Spirit

"Art is not the bread but the wine of life."
JEAN PAUL RICHTER

Pink Mandala

Moonlight Family Dream

"*Tread softly! All the earth is holy ground. It may be, could we look with seeing eyes. This spot we stand on is a paradise.*"

CHRISTINA ROSSETTI

Red Cats

Purple Gold Mandala

"If you would be loved, be lovable."
OVID

Strawberry Fields

Women's Movement

As an artist, especially when coloring in, your awareness
will expand into feeling—whether it is pain or joy—and your soul
will become enhanced and enriched.

Moon Walk

Swan Song

"*Know yourself to improve yourself.*"
AUGUSTE COMTE

Visions of Kauai

QUOTES ARE TAKEN FROM:

RUMI was a thirteenth-century Persian poet, theologian, and Sufi mystic.

BLACK ELK was a famous holy man, traditional healer, and visionary of the North American tribe of Oglala Lakota (Sioux).

PAUL GAUGUIN was a French Post-Impressionist painter whose work only became revered after his death.

THICH NHAT HANH is a Zen Buddhist monk, author, and one of the leading spiritual teachers.

MOTHER MEERA is an Indian avatar, believed by her devotees to be an embodiment of the Divine Mother or Shakti.

CARL JUNG was a revolutionary psychiatrist and pyschotherapist. He is best known for having founded analytical psychology.

JEAN PAUL RICHTER was a German writer, known for his experimentation with Romantic formlessness in his novels.

CHRISTINA ROSSETTI was a Victorian poet who predominantly wrote in a Romantic style.

OVID was a Roman poet whose work strongly influenced more recent European art and literature.

AUGUSTE COMTE was a French philosopher and theorist. He was most prominently known as the originator of both positivism and sociology.

PAUL HEUSSENSTAMM

Paul Heussenstamm is a master painter of mandalas and other forms of spiritual paintings. He has painted and drawn over 1,000 mandalas and has taught worldwide for 25 years, as well as at his studio in California.

Since 1996, he has worked for the Chopra Center for Wellbeing, sharing his art at almost every major event that Deepak Chopra hosts. He is the sanctuary artist at the Agape International Spiritual Center in Culver City in California, which has 10,000 local members.

Publishing director Sarah Lavelle
Commissioning editor Lisa Pendreigh
Creative director Helen Lewis
Designer Emily Lapworth
Production director Vincent Smith
Production controller Stephen Lang

First edition for North America published in 2016
by Barron's Educational Series, Inc.

First published in 2015 by
Quadrille Publishing
www.quadrille.co.uk

Quadrille is an imprint of Hardie Grant.
www.hardiegrant.com.au

All inquiries should be addressed to:
Barron's Educational Series, Inc.
250 Wireless Boulevard
Hauppauge, NY 11788
www.barronseduc.com

ISBN: 978-1-4380-0838-7

Printed in China

9 8 7 6 5 4 3 2 1

For best results, colored pencils are recommended.